soho
theatre + wr

GW00374880

Soho Theatre Company

Shoreditch Madonna

by Rebecca Lenkiewicz

First performed at Soho Theatre on 6 July 2005

Shoreditch Madonna was commissioned as part of
Soho Theatre's Writers' Attachment Programme,
supported by the Harold Hyam Wingate Foundation.

Soho Theatre is supported by

 gettyimages

Performances in the Lorenz Auditorium

Registered Charity No: 267234

Shoreditch Madonna

by Rebecca Lenkiewicz

FRANCESCA ANNIS	**MARTHA**
ADAM CROASDELL	**NICK**
LEE INGLEBY	**HODGE**
LEIGH LAWSON	**DEVLIN**
ALEXANDRA MOEN	**CHRISTINA**
DANIEL RABIN	**MICHAEL**

Director	**Sean Mathias**
Designer	**Paul Burgess**
Lighting Designer	**Jason Taylor**
Sound Designer	**Fergus O'Hare**

Production Manager	**Nick Ferguson**
Stage Manager	**Sarah Buik**
Deputy Stage Manager	**Sharon Cooper**
Assistant Stage Manager	**Geraldine Mullins**
Chief Technician	**Nick Blount**
Chief Electrician	**Christoph Wagner**
Lighting Technician	**Mark Watts**
Scenery built and painted by	**Robert Knight Ltd.**

Press Representation	Nancy Poole (020 7478 0142)
Photography	Getty Images

Rebecca Lenkiewicz would like to thank:

Sean Mathias, Dinah Wood, Nina Steiger,
Jon Lloyd, Abigail Morris, Max Stafford-Clark –
and Peter Quint for permission to steal (again)

Biographies

Writer

Rebecca Lenkiewicz Writer

Rebecca was part of Soho Theatre's Writers' Attachment Programme in 2004. Her most recent play, *The Night Season*, opened at the National Theatre in July 2004. She received the Critics' Circle's Most Promising Playwright Award and was nominated for the Charles Wintour Award for Best New Writing in the Evening Standard Awards and the Susan Smith Blackburn Award. Her first play *Soho – A Tale of Table Dancers* won a Fringe First at Edinburgh in 2000, played at the Arcola Theatre and toured Israel. Other writing credits include *Fighting For Words* (BBC Radio 4) and *Invisible Mountains* (National Theatre Education Department). As an actor, Rebecca has worked with the Globe, the National, the RSC and for film and television.

Cast

Francesca Annis *Martha*

Francesca's theatre credits include *Henry IV* (Donmar Warehouse and tour); *The Vortex* (Donmar Warehouse); *Blood* (Royal Court); *Hamlet* (American tour); *The Heretic* (London Stage); *Arms and the Man* (Windsor Theatre); *Romeo and Juliet, Troilus and Cressida* (RSC); *Month in the Country* (National Theatre); *Three Sisters* (Albery Theatre); *Mrs Klein* (National Theatre and Apollo Theatre); *Sienna Red* (English tour); *Rosmersholm* (Young Vic);

Lady Windemere's Fan (West End and tour); *Hamlet* (London and New York); *Hedda Gabler* (Plymouth and tour); *Ghosts* (Windsor and West End). Film credits include *Revolver* (dir. Guy Ritchie); *The Libertine* (dir. Laurence Dunmore); *Copenhagen* (BBC); *Milk* (dir. William Brookfield); *Debt Collector* (dir. Anthony Neilson); *El Rio De Oro* (Tresauro SA); *Under the Cherry Moon* (Warner Bros); *Dune* (dir. David Lynch); *Krull* (dir. Peter Yates); *Penny Gold* (dir. Jack Cardiff); *The Tragedy of Macbeth* (dir. Roman Polanski); *The Walking Stick* (Winkaast Films); *Big Mack and Poor Clare* (Atlantic United Productions) and *Gemmi* (Fanfare Films).

Adam Croasdell *Nick*

Adam's theatre credits include *Faithful Dealing* (Soho Theatre studio); *Romeo and Juliet* (English Touring Theatre); *Office Games* (Bill Kenwright); *Antigone* (Bristol Old Vic); *Perfect Days* (Wolsey Theatre); *Emma* (Tricycle Theatre); *Peter Pan, Anthony and Cleopatra* (National Theatre); *Mojo* (Market Theatre); *Bouncers* (Civic Theatre). Film credits include *Too Much Too Young* (Pensmith); *Avalanche* (Nu Image / Studio Eight); *Flyfishing* (Shooting Pictures); *Fatboy and Twintub* (Hypnotic Films); *Red Meat* (Rapid Blue) and *Tarzan – The Lost City* (Warner Bros). TV includes *The Project* and *Leonardo* (BBC); *Peak Practice* (ITV).

Lee Ingleby *Hodge*

Lee's theatre credits include *The Pillowman* (National); *A Midsummer Night's Dream*, *Cressida* (Almeida in the West End); *Drink, Dance, Laugh and Lie* (The Bush) and *Dreaming* (Royal Exchange); *About the Boy* (Royal Court). Film credits include *The Henchman's Tale* (Film and Music Entertainment); *Haven* (My World Entertainment); *Harry Potter III* (Warner Bros); *Master and Commander* (Far Side of the World Ltd/Fox); *Borstal Boy* (Hell's Kitchen); *Ever After* (Fox) and *Beer Goggles* (Compulsive Viewing). Television credits include *Hustle* (BBC/Kudos Films); *Early Doors, Danziel and Pascoe, The Dark Room, In the Red, Jonathan Creek, Nature Boy* (BBC); *Blue Murder* (Granada Television); *No Angels* (Channel 4); *Fat Friends* (Tiger Aspect); *Clocking Off* (Red Prods); *Impact* (ITV); *Nicholas Nickleby* (Company TV for ITV); *Spaced* (LWT for Channel 4); *Junk* (Zenith/BBC); *A Small Addition* (Hat Trick/BBC) and *Killer Net* (La Plante Productions).

Leigh Lawson *Devlin*

Theatre work includes: most recently, Dr Mirander in *Death and the Maiden*, King's Head Theatre. RSC: Oberon/Theseus in *A Midsummer Night's Dream*, dir. Adrian Noble; Loveless in *The Relapse*, dir. Ian Judge. RNT: *Yonadab*, dir. Peter Hall; *The Second, Mrs Tanqueray*, dir. Michael Rudman. West End Theatre: Lloyd in *Noises Off*, dir. Jeremy Sams and Anna Linstrom; Marc in *Art*, dir. Matthew Warchus and Thea Sharrock; Deeley in *Old Times*, dir. Lindy Davies; Antonio in *The Merchant of Venice*, dir. Peter Hall; Baldo in *A Touch of Spring*. In the USA: Lloyd in *Noises Off*; Antonio in *The Merchant of Venice* (Broadway); Sydney in Neil Simon's *Hotel Suite (Roundabout Theatre, New York)*; Horner in *The Country Wife* (Washington Shakespeare Company); *Barrymore* (Arizona City Theatre). TV: Lomax in *Travelling Man*; Kinsey in *Kinsey*; Logan in *Stick with Me Kid*; *Song of Songs*; *Tears in the Rain*; *Lace*; *Why Didn't They Ask Evans?*; *Disraeli*; *Queenie*; *Voice of the Heart*; *The Ring*; *Silent Witness*; *Heartbeat*; *Absolutely Fabulous*; *Coach*; *The Nanny*; *Phantom*; *The Captain's Doll*; *Journey into the Shadows*; *Charlie Boy*; *Deadline Madrid*; *The Small Assassin*; *Black Carrion*; *O'Pioneers*; *Battling for Baby*; *An Unsuitable Job for a Woman*. Film: *Casanova*, dir. Lasse Halstrom; *Silence Becomes You*, dir. Stephanie Sinclaire; *Being Julia*, dir. Istvan Szabo; *Madame Sousatzka*, dir. John Schlesinger; *Tess*, dir. Roman Polanski; *Love Among the Ruins*, dir. George Cukor; *Brother Sun, Sister Moon*, dir. Franco Zefferelli; *The God King*; *Ghost Story*; *Sword of the Valiant*; *The Tiger Lilly*; *Golden Rendezvous*; *The Devil's Advocate*; *The Sword and the Fire*. Directing: *The Cherry Orchard*; *Next Time I'll Sing To You*; *Noel & Gertie*; *The Restaurant*; *Make Us Believe It*; *If Love Were All*.

Alexandra Moen *Christina*

Alexandra's theatre credits include *Look Back in Anger* (Royal Lyceum Theatre); *The Seagull, The Merchant of Venice* (Chichester Festival Theatre); *The Hinge of the World* (Yvonne Arnaud Theatre) and *Macbeth* (Albery Theatre). Television credits include *Whatever Love Means* (Granada); *Falling* (YTV); *Midsommer Murders* (Bentley Productions) and *Foyle's War* (Greenlit Productions).

Daniel Rabin *Michael*

Daniel's theatre credits include *The Jerusalem Syndrome* (Soho Theatre); *Chicken Soup with Barley* (Nottingham Playhouse); *Achildi J's Final Hours* (Finborough Arms); *The Coffee Lover's Guide to America* (Chelsea Theatre); *Seven Sonnets of Michael Angelo* (Lyric Hammersmith); *The Last Sortie* (New End Theatre); *Corpus Christie* (Pleasance Theatre); *Untitled* (The Place); *Famous* (Wok Theatre, Vienna); *Un/Seen* (Mosaic Festival) and *Passionate Landscape* (Vienna Festival). Film credits include *Mind the Gap* (Tyler Films); *Two's Company* (Chahaya Films); *The Penalty King* (Twin Track Films) and *Suzie Gold* (Greenwolf Films). TV includes *Eastenders* and *Casualty* (BBC); *Money Can't Buy You Love* (Channel 4)

Creative Team

Sean Mathias *Director*

For theatre he has directed: *Bent* (Martin Sherman), *Uncle Vanya* (Anton Chekov), *Ghosts* (Henrik Ibsen), *Les Parents Terribles* (Jean Cocteau), *Design for Living* (Noel Coward), *A Little Night Music* (Stephen Sondheim), *Marlene* (Pam Gems), *Antony and Cleopatra* (William Shakespeare), *Suddenly Last Summer* (Tenessee Williams), *Servicemen* (Evan Smith), *Dance of Death* (August Strindberg), *The Elephant Man* (Bernard Pomerance), *Company* (Stephen Sondheim), *Antigone* (Sophocles), and *Aladdin* (Bille Brown).
On Radio: *Les Parents Terribles*. On Film: *Bent*. He has worked variously at the Royal National Theatre and in the West End (UK), the Kennedy Center and off and on Broadway (USA) and in numerous cities around the world including Paris, Sydney and Cape Town. Sean has written a number of plays including the award-winning *A Prayer for Wings* and the screenplay for the award winning BBC film *The Lost Language of Cranes*. Sean has won La Prix de la Jeunesse at the Cannes Film Festival, an Edinburgh Festival Fringe First Award, and in London the Critics Circle Award and the Evening Standard Award for Best Director; he has also been nominated for the Olivier and Tony awards. Later this year Sean will direct Annette Bening in *The Cherry Orchard*.

Paul Burgess *Designer*

Paul's recent designs include *Flush* (Soho Theatre); *The Most Humane Way to Kill a Lobster* (503); *Cancer Time* (503); *Much Ado About Nothing* (Globe, sets only); *One for the Road, Party Time* (BAC); *Have I None*

(Southwark Playhouse); *Peer Gynt* (Arcola) and *Choked* (tour). Other designs include the first production of Orton's *Fred and Madge* (OUDS, Oxford Playhouse) and various New York fringe shows. Assistant designing includes *The Ramayana* (RNT); *Twelfth Night* (Shakespeare's Globe US tour) and projects for Tara Arts. Film work includes five short films shot in Ghana and videos for various theatre productions. Paul has also created installation-based performances for The Arches, Glasgow, and The Junction, Cambridge. As co-founder of Scale Project he has worked on art-theatre crossover projects in Novosibirsk, Siberia and various UK locations. He also teaches design and video-making for the creative and performing arts charity Youth CREATE.

Jason Taylor *Lighting Designer*

Jason's recent and current credits include *Some Girls* (Gielgud Theatre); *National Anthems* (Old Vic); *Twelfth Night* (Albery Theatre); *Journey's End* (Comedy Theatre and national tour); *High Society* (national tour); *Lady in the Van* (national tour); *Madness of George III* (West Yorkshire Playhouse); *Us and Them* (Hampstead Theatre); *Hobson's Choice, Yerma* (Royal Exchange Theatre); *Abigail's Party* (New Ambassadors, Whitehall and national tour); *Pretending to be Me* (Comedy Theatre); *Little Shop of Horrors* (West Yorkshire Playhouse); *My Night with Reg/Dealer's Choice* (Birmingham Rep); *The Clearing* (Shared Experience); *Single Spies* (national tour); *Sitting Pretty* (national tour); *Pirates of Penzance* (national tour); *Office* (Edinburgh International Festival); *Hedda Gabler, Snake in the Fridge* (Royal Exchange Theatre); *The Dead Eye Boy* (Hampstead Theatre) and *Iolanthe, The Mikado* and *Yeoman* (Savoy Theatre). Jason has lit over 200 other productions including 14 seasons at the Open Air Theatre, *Kindertransport* (Vaudeville Theatre); *Rosencrantz and Guildenstern* (Piccadilly Theatre); *And Then There Were None* (Duke Of York's Theatre) and *Great Balls of Fire* (Cambridge Theatre).

Fergus O'Hare *Sound Designer*

Fergus's credits include *This Is How It Goes, The Cosmonaut's Last Message to the Woman He Once Loved in the Former Soviet Union, Henry IV* (Donmar Warehouse); *On the Ceiling* (Birmingham Rep); *Philadelphia Story, Aladdin, Cloaca, Hamlet, The Tempest, 24 Hour Plays* (Old Vic); *Someone Who'll Watch Over Me* (Ambassadors); *Hecuba* (RSC); *Dracula* (tour); *One Under* (Tricycle Theatre); *Anna in the Tropics* (Hampstead Theatre); *Vermilion Dream* (Salisbury); *Clouds* (tour); *Rookery Nook, Easter, Home, Candida, Singer, Serjeant Musgrave's Dance, Home, Candida, The Quare Fellow, Singer* (OSC); *Twelfth Night* (Albery) and *Shimmer* (Traverse). Credits in New York, Los Angeles and Sydney include *The Shape of Things, A Day in the Death of Joe Egg, Dance of Death, Noises Off, Electra* (Drama Desk Nominee) and *An Enemy of the People.*

● soho
● theatre + writers' centre

Soho Theatre Company is passionate in its commitment to new writing, producing a year-round programme of bold, original and accessible new plays – many of them from first-time playwrights.

'a foundry for new talent ... one of the country's leading producers of new writing'   *Evening Standard*

Soho Theatre + Writers' Centre offers an invaluable resource to emerging playwrights. Our training and outreach programme includes the innovative Under 11s scheme, the Young Writers' Group (15-25s) and a burgeoning series of Nuts and Bolts writing workshops designed to equip new writers with the basic tools of playwriting. We offer the nation's only unsolicited script-reading service, reporting on over 2,000 plays per year. We aim to develop and showcase the most promising new work through the national Verity Bargate Award, the Launch Pad scheme and the Writers' Attachment Programme, working to develop writers not just in theatre but also for TV and film.

'a creative hotbed ... not only the making of theatre but the cradle for new screenplay and television scripts'   *The Times*

Contemporary, comfortable, air-conditioned and accessible, Soho Theatre is busy from early morning to late at night. Alongside the production of new plays, it is also an intimate venue to see leading national and international comedians in an eclectic programme mixing emerging new talent with established names.

'London's coolest theatre by a mile'   *Midweek*

Soho Theatre Company would like to thank:

Aynsley China Ltd
Francesca Annis' hair by Louise Galvin and Brendon
at Daniel Galvin
Rose Marie Vernon
Teach Yourself Arabic course
donated by Hodder Education
Herbal smoking mixture kindly donated
by HONEYROSE Products Ltd, Ipswich
Carlsberg UK Ltd

● soho
● theatre + writers' centre

21 Dean St
London W1D 3NE
Admin: 020 7287 5060
Box Office: 0870 429 6883
Minicom: 020 7478 0136
www.sohotheatre.com
email: box@sohotheatre.com

The Terrace Bar

The Terrace Bar on the second floor serves
a range of soft and alcoholic drinks.

Email information list

For regular programme updates and offers,
join our free email information list by emailing
box@sohotheatre.com
or visiting
www.sohotheatre.com/mailing

Hiring the theatre

Soho Theatre has a range of rooms and spaces
for hire. Please contact the theatre managers on
020 7287 5060
or go to
www.sohotheatre.com
for further details.

Soho Theatre Company

The Soho Theatre Development Campaign

Soho Theatre Company receives core funding from Arts Council England, London. In order to provide as diverse a programme as possible and expand our audience development and outreach work, we rely upon additional support from trusts, foundations, individuals and businesses.

All our major sponsors share a common commitment to developing new areas of activity and encouraging creative partnerships between business and the arts.

We are immensely grateful for the invaluable support from our sponsors and patrons and wish to thank them for their continued commitment.

Soho Theatre Company has a Friends Scheme to support its education programme and work in developing new writers and reaching new audiences. To find out how to become a Friend of Soho Theatre, contact the development department on 020 7478 0111, email development@sohotheatre.com or visit www.sohotheatre.com

Sponsors   American Express • Angels, the costumiers • Arts & Business • Getty Images • TEQUILA\London

Major Supporters and Education Patrons   Anthony and Elizabeth Bunker • Tony and Rita Gallagher • Nigel Gee • Roger Jospé • Jack and Linda Keenan • John Lyon's Charity • The Regent Street Association • The Foundation for Sport and the Arts • The Harold Hyam Wingate Foundation

Trusts and Foundations   Anonymous • The Ernest Cook Trust • The Delfont Foundation • Hyde Park Place Estate Charity • The Kobler Trust • The Mercer's Company Charitable Trust • Leopold de Rothschild Charitable Trust • The Royal Victoria Hall Foundation • The St James's Trust • The Edward and Lois Sieff Charitable Trust • Unity Theatre Trust

Dear Friends   Anonymous • Jill and Michael Barrington • Jos Chambers • David Day • John Drummond • Madeleine Hamel • SoFie and Le'le' • Michael and Mimi Naughton • Oberon Books • Rick Russell, Final Cut Ltd • Diana Toeman • Jan and Michael Topham • Carolyn Ward • Piper Smith Watton

Friends   Thank you also to the many Soho Friends we are unable to list here. For a full list of our patrons, please visit www.sohotheatre.com

Registered Charity: 267234

Rebecca Lenkiewicz
Shoreditch Madonna

faber and faber

First published in 2005
by Faber and Faber Limited
3 Queen Square London WC1N 3AU

Typeset by Country Setting, Kingsdown, Kent CT14 8ES
Printed in England by Mackays of Chatham plc, Chatham, Kent

A CIP record for this book
is available from the British Library

ISBN 0–571–23007–5

2 4 6 8 10 9 7 5 3 1

Characters

Christina
in her thirties

Michael
in his thirties

Nick
in his thirties

Hodge
in his twenties

Devlin
in his fifties, Irish

Martha
in her forties

*The action takes place in a derelict art space
in Shoreditch and in a bedsit in Streatham,
London, 2005*

Act One

Christina's bedsit. It is small and basic but made feminine through various scarves and découpage. A figure is under the covers. A bedside table with some objects on it including dope and tobacco.

Christina is sitting on a wooden chair, dressed in a man's pyjamas. She sings:

Christina
'There is a green hill far away
Without a city wall
Where the dear Lord was crucified,
Who died to save us all.'

SCENE TWO

The Space. A cell-like room, derelict, an old, stained mattress. Michael is setting up a video camera and lights. Nick walks in with more bags. They are setting up throughout the scene.

Michael He's late.

Nick He's always late.

Michael Sit on the mattress and I'll focus.

Nick It's wet.

Michael It's just rain.

Nick smells the mattress and puts a bin-liner over it, then sits. Michael is focusing.

Talk to me.

Nick What about?

Michael Anything. Your mouth is just a hole now. Talk.

Nick That woman phoned me. The one who came into the shop. She wants me to go round to her place tomorrow night.

Michael We need to do more of this tomorrow. What does she want you to do?

Nick She's making a short. I'd only need to be there for two hours. Fifty quid. I could get Hodge a bike.

Michael Which woman you talking about?

Nick The one with the black dress and fur coat. Yesterday. She got a couple of films out.

Michael Uh-huh. You can move now.

Nick gets up. Hodge walks in and starts to help with setting up. There are noises offstage of banging metal.

Hodge He's here.

Michael Except he's not here, is he? Else I'd be talking to him.

Hodge He says he wants a chair now. A yellow chair. He wants to do it sat down.

Michael Where is he?

Hodge Checking the locks. Seeing if they're secure.

Michael They're not going to be bloody secure if he smashes them, are they? What do you have to do for this woman?

Nick She wants to film me sitting. With my back to her. Then she wants me to walk around in her room. Just the body doing different ordinary things.

Michael Naked?

Nick No. Nothing like that.

Michael You don't think you're being a bit naive?

Nick I think it's for her degree.

Michael So is it her arse or her thesis that you're attracted to?

Nick Neither.

Michael I'd fuck her for free anyhow, wouldn't you?

Nick No.

Michael Liar.

Nick There's no connection there.

Michael That's bullshit.

Nick It's not.

Michael So tomorrow she asks you where you do your work. Next day she comes round here. She stands in front of the window. Talks about Matisse and the angles in his bodies. Smokes a cigarette. Pearl choker, little black dress. Hair up like those French schoolteachers have it.

Hodge A chignon.

Michael Exactly. Turns her back to you. Slips her dress off. Shoulderblades like Anna Karina. She's looking at you now. Naked except for a pair of silk knickers. Pigeons in the roof are vibrating. Evening sun's just catching the nape of her neck. Then she opens her mouth ever so slightly and you say, 'I'm really sorry but I've got to go and stretch my canvas.'

Nick Yeah, well, it depends.

Michael On what?

Nick We might have made a connection while she was talking about Matisse.

Michael You're a windfucker, Nick.

Nick You're an omnifucker.

Michael No. I'm very selective in my conquests. Gaffer Hodge? I've never had an aristocrat. Always thought they'd be pretty good. All that repression. The women are sort of trained, aren't they?

Hodge Trained?

Michael Finishing school. Laying the table. The emphasis is on pleasing the man, isn't it? Good wife. Good cook. They're always bending over or on their knees.

Hodge It's actually the proletariat downstairs who are on their knees.

Michael She had that smell of fucking on beige leather car seats. Leading tall silent immigrants into bedsits.

Nick Which films did she rent?

Michael Can't remember.

Hodge *Eyes Without a Face* and *Throne of Blood*.

Nick What are they about?

Michael I'm not your pimp. Watch them if you want to impress her.

Nick Who are they by?

Hodge *Throne of Blood* is Kurosawa.

Nick Samurais?

Hodge Japanese version of *Macbeth*.

Michael It's fucking terrifying.

Hodge What? The bit at the end with the arrows?

Michael No, Devlin. What happened to him is fucking terrifying.

Hodge Going to prison?

Michael No. Losing it. How does someone become mediocre when they were such a fucking genius? What the fuck's he on about a yellow chair for?

Hodge Mm. We've been talking about this project for three months and he still doesn't know my name.

Michael It's a decision, isn't it?

Hodge But why us? Why choose to work with us?

Michael The galleries won't touch him any more. He's a fucking relic, isn't he?

Hodge He knows what's going on, though. We were just talking about Badiou and inaesthetics. He knows what people are up to.

Nick He doesn't know what any of us are up to. He hasn't once asked to see our work.

Hodge He must just have a good feeling about us. He's doing it by his instincts.

Michael No. He just knows that where a group of young blokes are, girls won't be far away.

Hodge You don't like him, do you?

The sound of footsteps coming up a stone stairway.

Michael I don't know him. But he's a sly fucker. I can't decide whether he's a shark or a pussycat.

Devlin enters. He is in his fifties, physically unkempt, bohemian but not tramp-like, with various carrier bags.

Devlin Who is a pussycat?

Hodge The locks are good, aren't they, Devlin? Strong?

Devlin Nothing is strong.

Hodge No.

Devlin The walls are solid. That's good. How many pussycats could you swing in here?

Michael Twelve if they had short tails.

Devlin And sharks?

Hodge Four.

Devlin Terrifying fucking animals. They never stop swimming, do they?

Hodge No. It's biological.

Devlin Human coffins for ever on the prowl. Acoustic?

Hodge As you find it.

Devlin Then it'll do, boys, eh? I'll need a chair?

Michael We thought the mattress would be a good touch.

Devlin A chair. A yellow chair. I'll not sit on a billet with fuck stains on it.

Michael It's clean. Just old.

Devlin Is it blood?

Michael Rain.

Devlin Of a biblical shade.

Hodge I could get some sheets from my room.

Devlin No. I'll not sit on the edge of other people's mortality.

Hodge I could go downstairs and get some yellow crates from the alleyway.

Devlin If I had an affection for crates I would have been a milkman. Cowboys.

Nick What?

Michael You didn't say anything about a canary-coloured chair. We've been asking you for weeks what you might need.

Devlin I said it tonight. I told –

Hodge Hodge. Tristan Hodge.

Devlin Yes.

Michael But that was just now.

Devlin I thought the work we were doing was of a spontaneous nature?

Michael It is.

Devlin So get me a fucking chair. Now.

Michael We could get one for tomorrow.

Devlin I would like one for tonight.

Michael Let's just forget the filming, then.

Pause. Michael starts to dismantle the camera stand.

Devlin Wait. (*He opens up his wheelie-bag and produces a foldable yellow chair from it.*) It's lucky the Indians came prepared, eh, boys? Were you never in the Scouts?

Michael sets up the chair in the right place and Devlin sits on it.

Michael Okay. Let's just do a rehearsal.

Devlin readjusts himself.

Devlin I want no rehearsal. My whole life has been a fucking rehearsal.

Michael Okay. Just say a few words for level, Devlin.

Devlin I'd like to thank my mother for her exquisite indifference, my agent for perpetually pissing on me and God for creating woman.

Michael starts filming.

Michael Perfect. We're recording then.

Devlin My name is . . . No matter what my name is. Call me? Call me anytime.

Devlin laughs and strikes a good sitting pose for the camera.

SCENE THREE

Three a.m. Christina's bedsit in semi-darkness. Christina is curled up in bed with her back to us, next to 'Charlie' under the covers. She wears a black dress and pearls. She sits up on the edge of the bed in a state of insomnia. She lights a candle and starts to roll a joint.

Christina Charlie? Sorry. I can't sleep. Liam is drinking on our doorstep again. He just sits there and watches. Like a boy in a playground. He looks ten years older in the last six months. As if the alcoholic calendar is different to ours. He's only your age. You can see the blood through his skin now. He's started to walk like a boxer after a fight. Or a cowboy. Before a fight. Or a comedian who has no fight in him at all. I keep thinking that's how Jesus would be if he came back. Outcast. Sat on a step. By himself. Watching. Sorry. I'll stop talking soon. Night, Charlie.

The Space. Devlin's recording continues. Michael films him whilst Nick and Hodge watch.

Devlin I am not a talking picture. I am a fragment like yourself. I smell rank when I am terrified. Unctuous when aroused. The hair on my chest is the texture of iron filings. I have no memory of being hairless. And no desire to return to a depilated state.

Michael Do you want to talk about your relationship to Joseph Beuys?

Devlin No. I want to talk about myself. I have caressed sirens off the edge of ships while their sisters ate away my spine.

Michael Where would you put your work in relationship to Derrida?

Devlin We are a band of hunters, gatherers. Emotional magpies, vampyrs. Cut. There is a sound, no?

Michael Pigeons. In the roof.

Devlin A child.

Nick No.

Michael No.

Hodge No.

Devlin There is the concrete sound of a child. Behind the walls.

They all listen. Rain and pigeons can be heard.

Michael No.

Nick No.

Devlin In pain.

Devlin goes to the wall and touches it. Puts his back to it and listens to it. Comes away from it.

You have the list of participants for the weekend?

Michael refers to his notebook. Hodge knows it by heart.

Hodge Yes. Anna Heartstar. Aerialist.

Devlin Good.

Hodge Brian Cafolla. Dramaturg.

Devlin Fuck.

Michael Love Harlow. Poet. Didi Amin.

Devlin Who?

Michael You worked with her before. Geraldine Jones. Welsh. She's changed her name.

Devlin Ah yes. Poor Geraldine.

Michael Ten in total. Most of them are artists.

Hodge A few of them have been hypnotised before.

Devlin We should aim for twelve. Two more. Women.

Hodge Why women?

Devlin Because they smell sweeter. We can light the fires?

Hodge Yeah. We've got wood from the skips. Chopped. Downstairs.

Devlin Feels like a house in the forest. Leave me now, boys. I want to listen.

Michael We should get some more down on tape.

Devlin Should we? I am a man, not a machine. You could buy a dozen bottles of claret if you want to be useful. Doesn't have to be expensive. I know you're not the White Cube. Nor would ever want to be, eh, boys? This is a good space. It is very present. I'll join you downstairs in a while. I'll need some petty cash later. For research purposes. Leave the camera if you would, please.

Hodge Watch out for the stairs. They're slippery with the rain. It's the pigeons.

Devlin I'd rather have pigeon shit on the stairs than elephant shite on the walls. Don't worry about me. I have a good nose for excrement.

Hodge, Michael and Nick leave. Devlin produces a small bottle of vodka from his coat and a glass. He pours a drink and raises it to the walls.

Are you there? Of course you're there. You're always fucking there.

SCENE FIVE

Christina's bedsit. She turns on a lamp which gives a little light and sits back on the bed next to 'Charlie', who is under the covers. She drinks water.

Christina It still smells like school in the bathroom. Like TCP. I tried to take those mirrors off but they're fixed. If I lie down will you touch my back with your hand? Your hand feels bigger than my ribcage some nights. Will you trace my dinosaur-skeleton spine with your nicotine fingers? Please? Please. Thank you. How's your leg? Thank you. For being so kind.

She lies down next to 'Charlie'.

SCENE SIX

Devlin is recording himself. He is very drunk by now. His face might be relayed huge and iconic on a backcloth.

Devlin I have been severed from the art world like a dismembered limb. Skin still fluttering like pink ribbons as the leg is torn from the hip socket. I no more want a retrospective than a testicular tumour or thrombosis. I have as little desire to show my work as my genitals. I am not the long-lost twin of the loitering flasher who displays his hanging puzzled scrotum from behind his tired trench coat. I have been living in the shadows. Chiaroscuro. Where the light is kinder. I have forgotten the texture of early morning light. I hope to retreat from this space changed. Dignified. Ashamed. Beheavened. Cut. I can hear you. Come out, come out, wherever you are. I'll count to ten. One . . . two . . . three . . . four . . .

SCENE SEVEN

Outside the Space. There are some yellow crates. Martha is sitting on one of them. She has an A to Z in one hand. With her other hand she is feeling her heartbeat. Hodge comes out of the shadows and shocks her.

Martha Jesus!

Hodge Sorry. Sorry. I didn't mean to scare you.

Martha You made me jump.

Hodge Are you alright? Are you looking for somewhere?

Martha No, I'm fine.

Hodge Oh, right. I just came down for something that's . . . It's actually underneath where you're sitting.

16

Martha gets up.

Hodge Sorry. I didn't mean to disturb you. Are you looking for the art space?

Martha Yes. Are you part of it?

Hodge I am, yeah.

Martha Oh. Right. I need to speak to Devlin. The painter. I wanted to do the weekend forum. He's taking it, isn't he? Do you know him? Is he there?

Hodge Yeah, he's upstairs. I wouldn't call it a forum, though, else he'll start shouting. I'll take you up to him.

Martha No. Actually. I'll come back.

Hodge He's not in the middle of anything.

Martha No. I'll come by tomorrow. Are you alright?

Hodge Yeah.

Martha Just you seem terribly nervous.

Hodge No. I'm always like this. I prefer to think of it as being alert.

Martha To what?

Hodge Potential hazards. You know. Men at bus stops. Moths in my room. Women.

Martha Women doing what?

Hodge Anything, really. Shall I give him a message?

Martha Tell him a ghost came by to see him.

Hodge Okay. (*He starts to go.*) You should be careful round here. This time of night it can get a bit . . .

Martha A bit what?

Hodge . . . heated.

Hodge starts to go but Martha remains seated.

Are you waiting for someone?

Martha We're all waiting for someone, aren't we?

Hodge nods and leaves.

SCENE EIGHT

The Space. Devlin is drunk.

Devlin One hundred and sixty-five, one hundred and sixty-six , one hundred and sixty-seven, sixty-nine, sixty-nine . . . fuck . . . one thousand and one, one thousand and two. Nights, days, fuck it . . . There's a clock in the bar around the corner. Big fucking megalithic thing and it shows how many seconds are left before closing time. Counts them down. Very fucking loud it is. You might like it. Will I show it to you? Are you coming out or not?

He folds into himself.

SCENE NINE

Christina's bedsit. Christina gets up off the bed leaving 'Charlie' asleep. She is in a state of sleepwalking.

Christina Charlie. Charlie. You've got to get up now. It's time to get up. You have to get your train to Liverpool, sweetheart. Your appointment's at eleven. Charlie. Charlie, come on. You can't miss it. They'll fuck you around even more if you don't get there. Charlie.

She pulls back the covers and reveals 'Charlie', who is simply pillows. She takes down the pillows and lies with them on the floor as if they were a person.

The Space. Martha is waiting. She is looking through a large coffee-table art book on Devlin's work. Michael comes in with two takeaway teas.

Michael Sorry. I had to go outside for them. And there was a queue. Hodge had locked his room.

Martha What?

Michael The kettle. Mugs. They're in Hodge's room.

He gives her a tea.

Martha Oh. Thanks. That's great. I didn't even know this book existed.

Michael Yeah. Devlin's very big in Germany. Sugar?

Martha Thanks.

He gives her a little cafe packet of sugar.

Got a . . .?

Michael Spoon. No. Pen?

Martha No, you're fine. It's a huge space. You've made it beautiful downstairs.

Michael Yeah. We do the big shows down there. Smaller events up here.

Martha Is it just your own work?

Michael No no. We've had about thirty shows since we've been here. All different artists.

Hodge comes in carrying a shop mannequin.

Hodge It's you.

Michael Hodge, this is Martha. She's going to do the weekend forum. What did you lock your room for?

Hodge No reason. Martha.

Michael You two know each other?

Martha No, we've never met before.

Hodge No? No.

Martha Who's your friend?

Hodge That's a big question, isn't it?

Michael Hodge rescues things. We've had cats, dogs, drunks. We rehoused a crow here last Christmas, didn't we?

Hodge Oh yes. Rip. Till his wing got better.

Michael We were making a film on Dartmoor last summer and we found Hodge trying to put a sheep in the van.

Hodge Yeah, I thought it was lost. Or abandoned.

Michael Do you know Devlin?

Martha I do. I went straight from a convent school to his teaching me at St Martin's. I was the only one who used to blush in life drawing.

Hodge You were touched by nuns? Sorry. Taught by nuns?

Martha Taught and touched. I was a lamb to the slaughter. Is she going to be part of your work?

Hodge What? I'm doing a project on control versus spontaneity. I thought I might use this as a map of human . . . something. What do you think of Devlin's work?

Martha He was amazing. Then he got scared.

Devlin enters. He is carrying various newspapers.

Devlin Who is scared?

Martha You, Devlin. You must be fucking terrified.

Devlin Is it you?

Martha You're thinner.

Devlin You're older.

Martha Yeah. Thank God.

Devlin Leave us alone together, would you, boys? Please. Please?

Hodge Tristan and Michael.

Devlin Yes, of course. Tristan. Mickey. Go and look for Iseult and Minnie. They're out there somewhere. It's only a question of time, your locating them.

Michael See you again, Martha.

Martha I hope so. Goodbye, Hodge.

Hodge Yes.

Hodge and Michael leave. Devlin goes to Martha. He touches her face. He puts his hand gently around her neck.

Devlin Marta. Marta. God. I trust my senses less and less these days. But it's you.

Martha It is.

Devlin Twelve years, is it? Christ. And you found me here in Fagin's den with the Fournier Street Irregulars. That's incredible. I've been living in Bulgaria.

Martha I know.

Devlin Did you imagine I'd been devoured by wolves?

Martha No. I thought you'd make friends with them.

Devlin I did. I felt very at home with the extraordinary sounds they made at night. I'm sure we'd all be healthier and happier if we were permitted to howl at the moon like they do without an ASBO being issued by the neighbours next door. It's a fantastically beautiful country, Marta. The forests.

Martha I know. I went there. For a holiday.

Devlin You did? When were you there?

Martha About six years ago.

Devlin You should have looked me up.

Martha You didn't leave a forwarding address. Are you going back?

Devlin No. I had a dalliance out there with the wife of a local mafia man. My choice was London or a meat hook. I was quietly surprised at my suddenly profound desire to stay alive and experience more of the same repetitions. It's good to see you, Marta.

Martha I've put my name down for your weekend.

Devlin No. No, you mustn't do that.

Martha Why not?

Devlin It's boredom on a plinth.

Martha They all seem excited about it.

Devlin Those boys would get excited over a dog pissing against a tree. Why are you here?

Martha I heard about Charlie.

Devlin I thought that must be it.

Martha It suddenly felt important to forgive you.

Devlin Thank you. I've no idea what for, but thank you. Are you still painting?

Martha No. I found it too flat. It reminded me of you. Why did Charlie do it?

Devlin Drugs. He was injecting three times a day. I think he was simply tired. Very tired. (*Pause.*) It's always awkward how much time one allots to the dead, isn't it? Are you seeing someone?

Martha Yeah. He's twenty-seven.

Devlin A boy-child. Wonderful. I'm impotent now, you know.

Martha My God. Is that a blessing or a curse?

Devlin It depends whose side you're on. Actually it's somewhat of a release.

Martha So how do you find your way around without your cock?

Devlin I had to buy an *A to Z*.

Martha I wrote you so many letters.

Devlin You did.

Martha I thought you'd be lonely in prison.

Devlin I was.

Martha No. You're never lonely.

Devlin I'm always lonely, Marta. Don't rob me of my artist's badge. What you mean is I'm rarely alone. Your letters were received with open arms. But you can't fuck an envelope.

Martha So who did you fuck?

Devlin A couple of the boys there. One was the spitting image of Donatello's David. Mouth like a sewer. The contrast beguiled me.

Martha What happened to the girl you went inside for?

Devlin No idea. But less of the girl. She was fifteen. Perhaps she became a solicitor. How is your work?

Martha Good. I'm working on a series of sculptures about mirror images.

Devlin Metal?

Martha Wood. I'm using a lot of found objects.

Devlin And you're making a decent living? That's fantastic.

Martha Don't you want to know what they're about?

Devlin We'd probably need a week, wouldn't we? But someone's buying them?

Martha There's a gallery which sells them. 'Skin Four'.

Devlin The one under the arches?

Martha Yes.

Devlin Tsk tsk, Marta.

Martha What?

Devlin Come on. I met them at one of their openings. Couldn't see the paintings for all the fucking sushi and asahi.

Martha Nothing wrong with throwing a good party. You went to it.

Devlin Only because the booze was gratis. Pseuds fucking corner, isn't it? All they can do is pixellate. Just their names. Illy. Miko. Kat. They sound like a Japanese boy band and they all hail from Willesden fucking Junction. How much of a cut do they take?

Martha Fifty per cent.

Devlin Thieving little office-boy pricks. All they can do is pixellate. Christ, London's gone to the dogs. Where are you living?

Martha Bayswater.

Devlin We used to visit the cafés along there. I'd smoke a hookah and we'd read Rumi's poems together.

Martha That wasn't me. That was someone else.

Devlin Ah. Well, it should have been you. You haven't found religion, have you, Marta?

Martha No.

Devlin What have you found?

Martha looks at some sketches around the room.

Martha You. I've found you.

She looks at him.

Devlin You have. This is perfect. I'll go and get a few bottles in and we'll have a proper old restoration gossip, shall we? I actually gave the last of my funds . . . to the boys. They struggle, you know, with the space and all. I mean, if you provide for tonight I'll do the honours next time. Tomorrow. Whenever.

Martha gives him some money. He touches her neck as if drawing her.

Don't move! I used to say that for effect to you. But I mean it now. Stay. Yes?

Martha I'll stay. At least until you get back.

He kisses her cheek and rushes out. Martha sits.

SCENE ELEVEN

Christina's bedsit. Christina is checking her appearance and now puts a black scarf over the mirror to cover it. The bell rings. She presses an intercom buzzer and opens the door a little. She puts Bach on the tape recorder. Nick knocks at the open door.

Christina Hi. Thanks so much. For coming round.

Nick Hi. Nick.

Christina Great. Come in. Sit down.

Nick Thanks.

He sits. She switches off the music.

Christina Drink?

Nick Lovely.

Christina What would you like?

Nick You got some white wine?

Christina No. No. I have Pilsener? Or lemonade?

Nick Pilsener. Great.

Christina Do you want a glass or is a tin okay?

Nick Tin's good. So you're making a short film? What's it about?

Christina I prefer not to talk about my work, if that's okay.

Nick Fine. I'm the same.

Christina You don't like talking about the video shop?

Nick We're all temporary at Solaris. The wages go into an art space that we run.

Christina Yes, I know. We have a mutual friend. Devlin.

Nick Uh-huh. Yeah, he's doing some work with us at the moment.

Christina I don't really know him. We only met the once. He's a friend of a friend. What's he like?

Nick He's the last of the bohemians.

Christina Is he? Here's to them.

She gives him a beer and puts a glass ice bucket next to him.

Nick Cheers. (*He picks up a video from the table.*) *Throne of Blood*. Brilliant. Best filming of Shakespeare I've seen. Fantastic.

Christina It's not Shakespeare though, is it?

Nick Isn't it?

Christina The language is so sparse.

Nick Yeah.

Christina I like the arrows at the end.

Nick Yeah, they're amazing.

Christina What did it make you think of?

Nick The arrows? . . . Death.

Christina They always made me think of a hedgehog.

Nick Yeah? Yeah, I can see that. Do you share with someone?

Christina What?

Nick Nothing. Can I smoke in here?

Christina No. I mean yes. I thought you were minding if I, asking if I minded.

Nick Do you have an ashtray?

Christina I must have one. I do. I know I do.

Nick I've found one.

Christina Good.

Nick offers Christina a cigarette but she shakes her head. He lights up and they both sit down.

Can I ask you something? Hypothetically? How much would you charge to stay with someone for the night?

Nick What?

Christina It's the exchange of money for bodies. It fascinates me.

Nick I'd only stay with someone because I wanted to.

Christina Absolutely. But there's something rather wonderful about money on a bedside table, don't you think? I never married anyone.

Nick No?

Christina No. My hands are clean. (*She puts her hands into the ice bucket.*) It's good for the circulation. Geisha girls had to do this for hours. They started to bind girls' feet when they were six years old. A little mound of cracked child bones that they could only hobble around on like a broken doll. Men can be very brutal, can't they?

Nick They can.

Christina Don't take any notice of me if I say something awol. I took a shitload of drugs last week.

Nick That's brilliant. That's fantastic. What did you take?

Christina I tried to kill myself.

Nick Oh.

Christina Sorry. Has my suicide status unnerved you?

Nick No. No, it hasn't.

Christina The film's about a man in a green jumper. Faceless. I'll talk you through it later.

Nick Right. (*Pause.*) Why did you do it?

Christina Why? I didn't do it, did I? It's statistical, actually. I was reading about it. Men tend to do the deed whereas women are often crying out for help. The Americans have got this new prescription for depression. For people who live by themselves. They're told to put a video next to their bed and when they wake up they're supposed to switch it on and watch the person on screen for an hour before getting up. I was missing someone.

Nick Who are they watching?

Christina Anyone. As long as they're talking. About anything. It's supposed to form an impression of company. What do you think?

Nick It's the loneliest thing I ever heard of.

Christina Yes. But if it was the right tape?

Nick Do you have friends? Family in London?

Christina No. I've only got Charlie.

Nick Charlie?

Christina Yes. But he's dead. Yes. Charlie's dead.

Nick I'm sorry.

Christina Why? You didn't kill him, did you?

Nick No.

Christina No. No, he 'killed himself'. Three weeks ago today. Morning is the most popular time for it. And spring is the most favoured month. I suppose that if you feel that removed, it must just seem unbearable to watch things grow, mustn't it?

Nick Yeah.

Christina There's an apple blossom tree next to the bathroom window. And when I found him . . . do you mind me talking about this?

Nick No. Of course not.

Christina I came home and everything was switched on. The television. Sound down. The iron. All the lights. Radio. Anything electrical. I was planning to use the film we make to wake up with in the morning. Would you mind if I did that?

Nick No. No, I don't mind.

Christina Thank you. Do you mind? Really? Because I could ask somebody else. There's this man, Liam, who often sits on our step and I'm sure he'd do it.

Nick You didn't tell me about the tree. Outside the bathroom.

Christina Oh. Yes. It was just that petals from the blossom had flown in through the window and they were all over the floor and in the bathtub. Like confetti. It looked like a couple had stood in the bath and had been married there. Except they hadn't. He was hanging there with these petals under his feet.

Nick I could stay. Tonight. On the floor. If that would help you.

Christina Why would you do that?

Nick Why not?

Christina Won't someone miss you if you don't return?

Nick Possibly. I'll text her. Tell her that I'm playing poker.

Christina Do you lie to her?

Nick Sometimes.

Christina Why?

Nick Because women are so beautiful. I'll need to get some more cigarettes.

Christina Take the keys. Don't ring. Just come in. But put a scarf on. It's cold out there.

Nick I'm fine.

Christina Please. You might get ill. And if you borrow the scarf you have to come back.

Nick What's your name?

Christina Christina. Please. For me. Wear this. For protection.

She puts a woolly scarf around his neck and knots it in a familiar way.

SCENE TWELVE

The Space. Devlin and Martha are finishing a second bottle of wine. They are both a bit drunk.

Devlin Can I see your legs?

Martha Fuck off.

Devlin You've not become a prude, Marta?

Martha I'm not showing you my fucking legs.

Devlin I want to see if they've changed. Mine are repulsive now. Arterial. Varicose. Like a view from an aeroplane. And I'm losing my memory. It worries me. When I remember to worry about it. Do you remember things?

Martha Yeah. Every freckle on your shoulder.

Devlin Repulsive things.

Martha You always were a physical fascist.

Devlin Ruskin disowned his own wife for less.

Martha Do you remember our first date? You pulled me into that black cab?

Devlin No.

Martha Yes you do. You held my hand tight against your velvet trousers and you had a huge erection.

Devlin Halcyon days.

Martha I thought it was cancer. I burst into tears 'cos I thought you liked me enough to tell me you were terminally ill.

Devlin You look beautiful, by the way.

Martha Who found Charlie?

Devlin Fuck . . . His girlfriend. He hung himself from a pipe in the bathroom.

Martha Shit. I keep seeing him as a little boy since I heard about it.

Devlin He didn't leave a note. Just my name and number on a Rizla paper in his pocket. His girlfriend rang me. I sat on the edge of the bath staring at him. I've never seen a hanged man, Marta. He looked like a cartoon. Like the printing had fucked up with the lines and colours. His forearms were a deep dark red and his chin too. I was fascinated by this discolouration. I asked the sergeant about it. He said the blood had pooled. Pooled. It sounds so gentle, doesn't it? I harangued him when I saw him last. I was not kind to him.

Martha You were always good with him.

Devlin When he was a child. It was always a pleasure dragging him away from that fucking children's home. But when he became the confusion that was his adult life, I was impatient.

Martha You were his hero.

Devlin I didn't ask to be his fucking hero. Why did he write my name down, Marta? You've taken to wearing trousers? That's unfair.

Martha What?

Devlin You should give people permission to dream.

Martha Your whole life revolves around sex, doesn't it?

Devlin It has to. It's primal, isn't it? Every artistic expression is an instinct to procreate. Works of art should bear one universal title: 'Fuck me, please.' They could print it in Latin if it offended.

Martha Could it not read 'Love me, please'?

Devlin Loving. Fucking. It's the same thing. Everyone I have fucked I have loved, Marta. For a moment. Or a minute. Or a month. I think my problem is only temporary. I'm reading a book about it. They keep talking about men in their caves, don't they? What they omit to mention is that some of the most beautiful paintings existent are at Lascaux.

Martha It used to make me cry, all those fucking manuals you read. Sex. Psychology. Female sensibility. You had one for everything, didn't you?

Devlin Except one for living. That one escaped me.

Martha You were impotent for a while when we were together.

Devlin No. Not so. I was intimidated by your affair with that African prince. Affected, not impotent. My last foray has changed her name to Didi Amin. Are people born that lost?

Martha Can you be reliable, Devlin?

Devlin God no. But if I can help. You know how discreet I am.

Martha You were the biggest bloody gossip of them all.

Devlin Possibly. But all our circle is dead now or in Wales so there's only the sheep to tell it to. So do you fancy a fuck for old times' sake?

Martha No. I really don't.

Devlin It was a joke. I told you I'm flaccid as a cherub these days.

Martha Why did you give up painting?

Devlin Brando is dead. Did you know? Can I take your hand?

She gives him her hand.

That's sweet. Very sweet. (*He smells it.*) Like all the perfumes of Arabia.

He sits down with her hand in his.

Will you put your hand on my head?

She puts it on his brow. He takes a couple of breaths then moves her hand to his groin.

Martha We lived a lot, didn't we?

Devlin We did. We did. Your hands were always so pale. Like Rodin's Cathedral.

Martha takes her hand away from his groin.

Martha What's happened to you, Devlin?

Devlin What's happened to us all?

Martha Seriously.

Devlin The lights go out, don't they? No more cerebral activity. No thinking allowed. Would you hold me, Marta?

She holds him in her arms.

Can I put my head in your lap? Listen to your stomach, like the old days? (*He moves into this position.*) I can hear your womb. Like the Red Sea. I can't paint any more, Marta. It's a very particular sensation. Like living with a stranger who is lodged inside my skin.

Martha Your pictures used to make my heart stop, Devlin. I'd look at them and cry, they were so honest.

Devlin I can't make sense of anything, Marta.

Martha How long was it before you could make sense of things after Hildy died?

Devlin separates himself from Martha.

Devlin Perhaps you should go.

Martha You never talked about it to anyone.

Devlin Fuck off. She died. She was my child. Her bones had not even become themselves. What more is there to say?

Martha Nothing. I should go.

Devlin No. Marta. Please. We're not fighting are we? Come here my compadre. My Shoreditch Madonna.

Martha You come here, Devlin.

Devlin I will. I've been invited. I don't know why mountains and Mohammed had such issues with movement.

He goes to Martha and puts his arms gently around her. She puts her arms around him. He kisses her gently.

Marta. You still smell of oranges, Marta.

He holds her very tight.

My Gio-fucking-conda. Anaconda gioconda.

He loses himself in her and now starts to kiss her and tries to undress her.

Marta. Sweet Marta. Will you be my mother, Marta?

He puts his mouth to her breast.

Sweet Marta. Are you my mother?

Martha pushes him off.

Martha Fuck off, Devlin! I'm not your fucking mother.

Devlin I wasn't for a moment implying you were. It was a metaphor, Marta. An invocation of the sexual matriarch.

Martha You're not even impotent, are you? It's just another line.

Devlin That's as much as you know. But I don't blame you. I did you a lot of damage.

Martha I did damage to myself. You had nothing to do with it.

Devlin I'm sorry my touching you was upsetting. I thought you might have changed.

Martha You're a cold bastard, Devlin.

36

Devlin I am. But I have no choice but to live a life consigned to me. Whereas you have chosen to spend a great deal of your adult existence chasing me. What does that say about you, Marta?

Martha I was in love with you. Love's a fever. And incredibly indiscriminate. And I wasn't fucking chasing you.

Devlin Quite so. Mea culpa. It's good that you're angry. Good to let it all out.

Martha Fuck off, Devlin. Why do you always make me feel like a patient? You've always been so fucking formulaic. Woman angry, antidote A. Woman aroused, antidote B.

Devlin Me? Formulaic? I've never been formulaic. But are you? Aroused?

Martha No. Most definitely absolutely not.

Devlin So what's next? Do you want to berate me for the crushing oppression of your childhood to which I was not in fact party?

Martha I never fucking chased you.

Devlin I never asked you to write to me in prison, Marta. You bleated of your own accord.

Martha Do people seriously pay money to spend a weekend with you? Because you used to go to piss-ups with artists who make them salivate? Christ, you're so full of shit.

Devlin You could probably go now. If you wanted to.

Martha I am going. I used to watch you paint. You were so fucking brilliant, Devlin. I went to see your show at Venice last year. I felt embarrassed for you. It didn't resemble anything connected to real emotion. It felt more like you were trying to piss and it was painful. It was arthritic. Like the brushes were strapped to your wrists with barbed wire. Felt less like painting than pissing blood and ice.

Martha exits. Devlin puts his head in his hands.

SCENE THIRTEEN

The Space. Nick is playing a drum. He is lost in the music and his thoughts. He is very much on his own.

SCENE FOURTEEN

Christina is in her bedsit. She is playing the film of Nick's back onto her body. She is wearing underwear so that the film projects onto her body and she moves with it. Nick might lie down in the film and Christina might lie down with him and 'hold' him.

Christina Charlie. How are you? There was another man here. In your space. I thought it might make you come back for me. If I bent over for him would you kick the door down? Hit him? Crush his head until he didn't exist. Would you kiss my neck, Charlie? My eyes? We wasted so much time, didn't we? I hate other people, Charlie. I hate anyone who doesn't want to wash your feet. I hate them. I won't stay here. It doesn't make sense. Any of it. I'll see you soon. Be with you. Soon. Love's fantastic, isn't it?

SCENE FIFTEEN

The Space. Hodge is talking to the mannequin whilst painting it. The dummy is on a plastic platform so that with his foot he can imperceptibly make her lean forward and back.

Hodge She smells like oranges. Did you notice that? Her skin is translucent. And the shape that her breasts made under her shirt. She's like the Venus de Milo. Plus arms. She looked very lost with her book of streets. I wish she'd get ill so I could look after her. Not very ill. Just a cold. Blanket. Lemsip. Copies of *Viz*. Or maybe *Vogue*.

SCENE SIXTEEN

The Space. There is a 'Teach Yourself Arabic' tape playing and Michael is repeating the phrases.

Tape Yes. *NaAhm.*

Michael *NaAhm.*

Tape No. *Laa.*

Michael *Laa.*

Tape Please point to the phrase in the book. *Ashir ilaal Ahibaara feel kitaab, lau samaHt.*

Michael *Ashir ilaal Ahibaara feel kitaab, lau samaHt.*

Nick enters.

Nick What you listening to?

Michael Arabic. The language of love.

Nick You're not going away, are you?

Michael Not if it involves going anywhere with myself, no.

He turns off the tape.

Nick You okay?

Michael Yeah. You?

Nick Yeah.

Michael How did it go with that woman?

Nick Okay. How's Devlin?

Michael I've got the feeling he's going to bolt.

Nick Why?

Michael Maybe it's just me. I feel like everything's going away.

Nick Right.

Michael We've been lucky for three years. Invisible. Could get moved on any time now.

Nick Yeah. We've always known that.

Michael What would we do? Find somewhere else around here?

Nick Maybe. There's the old brewery. Loads of room for us and Hodge.

Michael Yeah. But Hodge'll probably want to move south if he gets that teaching job.

Nick I stayed the night on her floor.

Michael Did you?

Nick Yeah. I don't think she slept. She was breathing heavily and moving around. I stayed awake all night listening. And then I kept imagining waking up next to her. Seeing her head on the pillow next to me.

Michael Decapitated?

Nick Piss off. You got any dope?

Michael Leather jacket next to my bed.

Nick Can I take some? I said I'd go round there tonight. It might help her to sleep.

Michael You shouldn't go round there again tonight. It's too keen.

Nick Her boyfriend just hung himself. It's not the time to be playing games, is it?

Michael Probably not the appropriate time to be trying to fuck her either.

Nick That's not what I'm going there for.

Michael Right. My mistake. I'm thinking of leaving the Space.

Nick What? Why?

Michael I just think it might be time to do something on my own.

Nick Why?

Michael Why not?

Nick Because we've been leading up to a big exhibition for the past three years.

Michael We can still do that.

Nick A minute ago you were saying we'd go to the brewery.

Michael I've gone off the idea.

Nick What?

Michael I want to have more time to paint. I didn't start this whole thing just to answer fucking emails.

Nick Me and Hodge are always offering to do it.

Michael It's not as simple as that, is it? You get into a dialogue with people. You can't suddenly say, oh, my mate's taking over now. I'm the only one who knows what's going on with everyone.

Nick Because you won't let us touch it.

Michael Yeah. Probably. Possibly.

Nick You're not really thinking of leaving, are you?

Michael No. Not really.

Nick You okay?

Michael Yeah. Cabin fever. I'd better check on Devlin. Good luck with the merry widow.

Michael leaves.

SCENE SEVENTEEN

Christina's bedsit. Nick is lying on the floor. Christina is in bed. She seems to wake up. Her eyes are open but she is sleepwalking. She goes over to Nick and touches him gently.

Christina Hey. Did we fight?

Nick Mm? What? No.

Christina Why are you sleeping here?

Nick You asked me to stay again. Do you remember?

Christina No. Sorry. Was I horrible?

Nick No.

Christina I didn't mean it.

Nick What?

Christina Whatever I said. Sweetheart. Is your leg okay?

Nick Yeah, it's fine.

Christina You took your pills for it?

Nick What?

Christina Let me see your leg, Charlie.

Nick I'm not . . .

Christina pulls back the blanket and looks at Nick's leg. She touches it gently. Kisses it.

Christina Come to bed.

Nick To bed?

Christina Yeah. Please.

She strokes his hair and his face and kisses his face.

Is that nice?

Nick It's lovely.

She takes off her shirt and puts his hand on her breast.

Christina That's yours.

Nick Yeah?

She moves his hand to different parts of her body.

Christina And that. And that. And this. It's yours.

Nick Christina . . .

Christina I remember us fucking right here. I had bruises on my arms because you held me so tight. Beautiful sea-green imprints of your fingers on my skin. Do you remember? Fucking me here? Very slowly. Then very hard.

Nick does not reply.

Do you remember Charlie? Do you?

She kisses him.

Nick Yeah. Yeah, I remember.

Christina Come to bed. We never fuck any more. Come to bed and fuck me. Please. Please.

Nick Okay.

Christina How? How will you fuck me?

Nick Very slowly. Then very hard.

Christina Yes, Charlie. Very slowly. Then very hard.

She takes his hand and leads him into bed. They get into bed. Touch each other gently.

Lights down.

Act Two

*Christina's bedsit. Christina is lying down on her bed
like a rag doll, splayed. Devlin is sitting on the floor.
He reaches for his vodka in his coat. He is exhausted.
Christina is as if drugged and in a semi-trance state under
hypnosis. She sings.*

Christina
'We may not know we cannot tell
What pains he had to bear,
But we believe it was for us
He hung and suffered there.'

She hums the tune.

Devlin Christina. Chrissy? Do you want a drink? Have
a drink, will you?

*Christina gathers the covers around her. She comes to,
sitting with a huge effort.*

Christina Do I have to give it back to you? From my
mouth?

Devlin You've gone under very deep, Christina. How are
you feeling?

Christina Worried.

Devlin What's worrying you?

Christina Charlie's leg. It's putrid. It smells, but I don't
want him to know that. If he was a soldier he'd be a
hero, wouldn't he?

Devlin He would. Did he ever talk about me, Christina?
About Devlin?

45

Christina He said that you were hiding from him. In a red room in Austria.

Devlin I want you to try and picture him. Can you see him now?

Christina Yes. He's surrounded by metal and they're shaving his hair. They're cutting off his toenails and they're writing on his body. His beautiful body. He looks thinner.

Devlin What are they writing?

Christina Words.

Devlin Can you read them?

Christina Gitane, tsigane, gypsy. They're letting his blood and writing that with it.

Devlin Are you with him?

Christina No. They've made me stay on a plastic chair. And I'm not allowed to stand up.

Devlin Have they tied you up?

Christina No. But I'm not allowed. And I'm wet. I've pissed myself. And my thighs are beginning to rub. I've got my hand up but they're not taking any notice of me.

Devlin Is he angry with us, Christina?

Christina He's fucking furious.

Devlin Why?

Christina Because we lied to him.

Devlin Both of us?

Christina Everyone. But especially me. And most of all you.

Devlin What did I lie about?

46

Christina You said you loved him, but you were lying.

Devlin Can you talk to him?

Christina No.

Devlin Why not?

Christina Because he's dead. Is why. Because he's dead. He be. He be. He do the police in funny voices. He be dead.

She starts to get upset.

Devlin I want you to lie back down and I'm going to bring you out of it.

Christina No. I want to stay with him.

Devlin I'm just going to bring you back gently.

Christina You can't make me. No one can.

Devlin Charlie doesn't want you to stay there.

Christina Fuck off. You're a liar, Devlin. You can't see inside his head. I'm staying where I can see him.

Devlin The state is temporary. Do you understand?

Christina Everything. Everything.

Devlin lights a cigarette.

They're cutting you up into tiny pieces, Charlie. Because you never fitted in they're trying to make a human jigsaw out of your flesh and make it fit this time. They're slicing you up like a dog off the streets. They're drawing plans to burn your skin and pull your teeth out. Because you wouldn't do what they told you to do. Because you wouldn't fill in the forms.

Devlin leans over her and puts his hand on her forehead. He closes her eyes. He kisses her brow. He whispers into her ear. She wakes as from a very deep sleep.

Devlin Are you alright?

Christina Mm.

Devlin You want a drink? Some water?

Christina No.

Devlin You were out for a long time. Do you remember what you saw?

Christina Charlie. He was lying down.

Devlin Nothing else?

Christina No. Was there something else?

Devlin No. No, there was nothing else.

SCENE TWO

The Space. Martha, Michael and Nick are sharing a bottle of wine. Martha and Michael are completely drunk and stoned. Nick is not. Hodge is drawing lines on the lower body of the mannequin.

Nick Do you think he meant it?

Hodge Who?

Nick Devlin. He said that it would be healing for her.

Michael No. He's probably filming her now. He's clicked his fingers and told her to start dancing round in her baby doll nightie.

Nick Stop it.

Michael It was a joke, Nick.

Nick You've got a sick sense of humour.

Michael No. I've just got an incredibly vivid imagination.

And if I didn't possess one we never would have moved into this building and created an empire.

Nick I'm going round there. Now.

Martha I would leave it for a while, Nick. She'll be fine.

Hodge If he's not back by midnight I'll come with you. Get a night bus over there.

Nick Will you, Hodge?

Hodge Yeah. It might even be dangerous to disturb them mid-flow. Like sleepwalkers.

Michael Hypnosis interruptus.

Martha What are you drawing, Hodge?

Hodge It's a map of ecstatic moments. Using hieroglyphics and the symbols from the Ordnance Survey.

Michael Did you trace symbols like that on your geisha girl?

Hodge What?

Martha Which geisha girl?

Hodge Nobody.

Michael We went to a Thai massage parlour for Hodge's birthday.

Hodge Michael. Don't. Sorry, Martha.

Martha Tell me about it, Hodge.

Hodge It's months ago. There's nothing to tell. I've forgotten.

Michael Falsification. He remembers it. Every detail. Bamboo chairs. Madame de Fleur.

Martha Who's Madame de Fleur?

Hodge Oh yeah. She was the woman there. She had orchids in her hair.

Martha Really?

Hodge Yeah. The whole place was like a launderette designed by Hokusai.

Martha Seedy?

Hodge No. No it was clean. It smelt of furniture polish. This Madame de Fleur sat us down and gave us all a bottle of beer and took our money. And there were these wooden slatted doors like to a saloon. And they swung open and these five girls walked out. They were all wearing identical short white coats like dental nurses. And they had these calf-length shiny boots on. Different colours. Red. Black. And she said to pick which one we liked and everyone said I should choose first so I pointed to the girl with yellow boots and she took my hand.

Martha Was she the loveliest?

Hodge No. I mean, they were all absolutely stunning. But I thought she probably hadn't chosen those yellow boots. I reckon she was left with them after everyone else had taken theirs. And I went in and she gave me a massage.

Martha And then what?

Hodge Then she asked if I wanted anything else. And I . . . I said yes I would like something else. Yeah. And that was it.

Michael Except you left out the best bit.

Hodge I don't think I did.

Michael So we've all gone into our little rooms and done the business and we come out and have another beer and there's no sign of Hodge. And we wait. And we wait.

And Madame de Fleur looks a bit puzzled, and she smiles and goes off to check that everything's okay.

Hodge And it was. It was fine. Everything was fine.

Michael She comes back and tells us that Hodge has been on his knees to this girl from the moment they stepped into that room. He's gone down on her for hours and he's not stopping until she comes. He hasn't fucked her at all.

Hodge starts to tidy up the room.

Martha That's fucking in my book, Michael. Pretty serious fucking.

Michael Yeah, but they just want you in and out there as quick as possible. It's a job. They don't want the secrets of the fucking Perfumed Garden.

Martha How was your girl, Michael?

Michael Yeah, she was great.

Martha Did you imagine she was anyone else while it was happening?

Michael No. Why would I?

Martha You were just saying you had a vivid imagination.

Michael Shall I get some more booze from Tadim's before it shuts?

Hodge There's a whole case downstairs, Michael. Devlin asked me to get one in.

Martha What colour boots did yours wear, Nick?

Nick Hey? Oh. Blue.

Hodge I'm going to make you a blue drink, Martha. A flaming sambuca. Have you ever had one?

Hodge starts to prepare a flaming sambuca for her.

Martha No.

Hodge You're meant to drink it when it's alight from someone's belly button while they lie down on a marble cocktail bar, but I think we might have to stick to mugs.

Hodge gives her the blue flamed drink which he has endeavoured to decorate.

Nick I'm going to have to go round there. What if he tries it on with her?

Michael Fuck's sake, Nick. She's over the age of consent.

Nick She's in a state.

Michael If that meant you couldn't have sex the whole of Britain would be celibate.

Nick Devlin fucked a fifteen-year-old, didn't he? He doesn't have boundaries, does he?

Martha Not especially. Alive is usually enough.

Michael You can't call what he did rape. They were seeing each other. In some countries she'd be married.

Nick Not in this country.

Michael No. Not on this particular blessed isle. And God bless Queen Bess. Why are you getting so fucking sanctimonious?

Nick Adolescents should have sex with people their own age.

Michael And colour? And creed?

Hodge I don't think Nick was advocating eugenics, Michael. He's concerned. About her state of mind.

Nick I'm just expressing my opinion.

Michael Actually you're expressing your own sexual tension.

Nick Fuck you.

Michael What? It was meant very lightly. Tongue-in-cheek.

Nick Maybe I don't want your fucking tongue in my cheek.

Michael You didn't object to it once upon a time, did you?

Nick Fuck off.

Michael Look, why don't you calm down or piss off, Nick? Take your soapbox for a walk.

Nick takes the wine bottle, drinks the remains and walks out.

He's gone. That's better.

Hodge puts a coat over the mannequin and gets his jacket and keys.

Hodge I'd better go and check that he's alright.

Michael Leave him, Hodge. Leave the upright citizen alone.

Hodge No. No, I'd better go.

Hodge exits.

Michael Sorry about Nick. He's a bit uptight.

Martha You act more like his lover than his friend.

Michael Do I? It's not intentional.

Martha How long have you been in love with him?

Michael Sorry? What?

Martha What made you fall for him?

Michael I didn't.

Martha Oh. Okay.

Michael Falling's involuntary, isn't it? It's about encountering a certain geography where your footing goes. Followed by your mind.

Martha And something happened between you?

Michael We spent a night together. Two years ago.

Martha And you're still waiting?

Michael I'm here. This is where I live.

Martha Loitering with intent, then.

Michael Possibly.

Martha Are you hopeful about it?

Michael Yeah. Hope's a terrible thing, Martha.

Martha It is. I always hoped that I'd become my real self when I was with Devlin. It never happened.

Michael I'm myself with Nick. We both are. It doesn't affect our relationship. We work together. Do everything together.

Martha Not everything.

Michael You think I'm mad?

Martha Anyone who's in love is mad. It's wonderful. Do you ever think about leaving?

Michael I do, yeah. Most days. Usually when I'm walking back here. And then I get distracted by how excited I am to be approaching home. Knowing he's here. In one of ten rooms. Or somewhere close by.

Martha You're in a trap.

Michael Yeah. And there's no fear of parting, 'cos we're not together. It's beautiful.

Martha I felt the same about Devlin. He was always bringing back other women. It was like I was living in a fantastic cage.

Michael You think I should move out?

Martha Not necessarily. Love is pretty damn rare. So what if it's not wanted? Doesn't stop you sending it out, does it?

Michael All that unrequited fucking *amore* floating around. It's got to be landing somewhere, hasn't it?

Martha On an exotic uninhabited beautiful island, I should think. Getting caught in palm trees and being examined by spider monkeys.

Michael No wonder they're so fucking animated. Why did you come to see Devlin?

Martha It's necessary. Unfortunately.

Michael You don't want to get back with him?

Martha God, no. I see myself with him in the past now as if it was a terrible silent film. I feel terribly protective over my younger self. Silly, isn't it?

Michael No. Not at all. What did he do that was so wrong?

Martha He wasted my time. And he wasn't kind. I used to lie in the next room and hear him through the walls. Bringing back girls. Always the same routine. Glasses. Cork popping. Lyrical speech pattern. Then the creaking noises. Plosives. Sometimes I even thought I could smell his sweat. What happened the night you and Nick got together?

Michael We'd done a lot of pills. Yeah. I'd given him a couple of 'e's. And it was very . . . memorable.

Martha Did you have sex?

Michael It was . . . intimate. And I don't actually believe you can feel something that intensely unless something's coming back to you as strong from the other person. You'd just feel embarrassed if you were feeling it by yourself, wouldn't you? Exposed. I don't think it can reach that intensity unless it's reciprocated, do you?

Martha No, I don't. Did you talk about it?

Michael No. Never. I hear him fucking the girls he brings back here. I don't actively listen. Well, I did once. (*He puts on music.*) Fuck Devlin. Fuck Nick. Fuck them all. I think we should dance. I think it's the only way. We should have been born as those marathon dancers, you know? If I was a woman, Martha, I'd want to look like you.

Martha If I was a man I'd want to look like you. Let's dance. Let's dance till I have to walk on your feet.

He puts on music and takes Martha up in his arms to dance.

SCENE THREE

Christina's bedsit. Devlin and Christina are drinking coffee, sitting on her bed.

Devlin Was there something wrong with Charlie's leg?

Christina Tracking.

Devlin Is what?

Christina If you inject and it's not pure then it can go

56

toxic. He'd had to buy some stuff on the street because they'd made a mistake with his prescription. When they cut out the septic area it left a hole in his leg. They put in four feet of wadding to fill the gap.

Devlin Shit.

Christina Why did you two lose contact? He was hurt that you'd lost touch with each other.

Devlin My daughter and Charlie were childhood friends. She died. I found it hard to spend time with him afterwards.

Christina Were they close?

Devlin Inseparable. Exquisite muddy savages they were. They got engaged when they were seven by biting into each other's knee until it bled. Teeth marks for weeks on Hildy's left knee. After the accident I felt like I was looking at a dead child every time I went round to take him out. He sensed it.

Christina How old was he?

Devlin Ten. The sharpest age. When your imagination is kicking against being an adult. When people, fuckers, are trying to rip the childhood out of you. He felt that change acutely.

Christina Was he there when Hildy died?

Devlin No. She drowned. In the sea. I was on the beach. Reading the fantasies of the Marquis de Sade. I was so concentrated on hiding my erection in the sand that I didn't notice what was going on. People carried her to me. And I knew something epic had happened. The sky had changed colour. Literally. A blue I had never seen before. She'd be your age now. You mustn't deify Charlie, you know.

Christina I'm not.

Devlin And his naming me wasn't some code for 'This was the man who sucked my cock when I was a boy and that's why I'm ending it all.'

Christina I know that.

Devlin He knew I'd understand. That there should be no sentiment. No fucking rhetoric or religious chocolate-box attachment to death. If a child dies, that is a tragedy. But Charlie wanted to go, and you should celebrate that with him.

Christina I can't bear that he was alone, Devlin.

Devlin We're all alone. It's just whether we choose to acknowledge it or not.

Christina I held his hand for a while before you all got here and it was like damp marble. They'd have lain him out on a slab afterwards, wouldn't they? No blanket, no grass. Like a fish they wanted to fillet.

Devlin Absolutely.

Christina Don't you feel any sadness about his death?

Devlin No. I was mercifully anaesthetised on a beach many years ago and some fucker forgot to take out the needle. I have no capacity to feel anything.

Christina Nothing?

Devlin Nothing. I'm empty, Christina. Feel.

He takes her hand and puts it against his heart, then on to his face and then to his leg. He kisses her hand and puts her hand to her breast, then touches it himself. He kisses her. Christina starts to take her cardigan off. Devlin stops her. He puts her cardigan back on her.

Christina I want to.

Devlin No. It's not the right time for you.

Christina You just said I should celebrate.

Devlin Sleep. You should sleep.

Christina Devlin. Please. I have to get rid of this image in my head. Of Charlie. Please.

He sits up next to her. The bell buzzes. They do not respond. It buzzes again. They sit in silence. Christina turns out the light. The bell buzzes again. And again. For a prolonged time. A short buzz. Then quiet. A stone is thrown up at the window.

Nick (*from outside, shouting*) Christina!

She does not respond.

Devlin!

No response.

Devlin, you fucker!

Another stone. Then quiet. Then the sustained sound of the buzzer. Quiet. One last short hopeless buzz. Then quiet.

Devlin Is it the Mormons?

Christina No. I thought it might be Charlie.

Devlin It's the other one. He must be fond of you.

Christina Then he's fond of a dead woman. Put your hands around my neck, Devlin.

He does.

Don't let me breathe.

He kisses her.

Stop my mouth. Don't let me breathe.

He kisses her.

59

SCENE FOUR

The Space. The main lights are out but various lights are on – a flickering fridge light, flashing bike lamps and street lamps. There is loud music. Hodge is sitting transfixed by the music and thought. Michael and Martha are drinking and dancing and are completely out of it. They are throwing themselves into strange dark music full of drums. Nick comes in and is telling Michael that he couldn't get into Christina's. Michael is abandoned and nodding and tries to kiss Nick lightly and passes a joint to him. Nick talks to Martha, who nods and dances. We hear none of their conversation. Nick sits down and stares at them. He gets up and walks out.

SCENE FIVE

Christina's bedsit. Christina is in bed. Devlin is next to her.

Devlin You were talking in your sleep.

Christina About what?

Devlin You said 'I'm scared it will go through to the bone, Charlie.' Then you said 'Thank you for making them smooth.'

Christina He used to shave my legs for me. I was anorexic when we first met and I was always terrified that the razor would sever a vein while I was shaving. So he'd fill that orange bowl with soapy water and he'd sit there and shave them for me. Very gently. By the light of the electric fire. He'd rest his head against my knees. It was the first time someone had really done something for me.

Devlin I should go. Martha will probably be hanging around the studio. Worrying about me.

Christina Yes. Thank you.

Devlin Stop fucking thanking me. I wasn't a magician at your birthday party.

Christina No. Sorry.

Devlin And stop apologising.

Christina Yes. Sorry.

Devlin Errol Flynn used to employ prostitutes. Can you imagine? Errol fucking Flynn? When they asked him why he'd do such a thing, he said he wasn't paying for the sex. He was paying for them to leave in the morning. (*Looking at the objects on the bedside table.*) Are these Charlie's things?

Christina Yes. Every time he came in he'd empty his back pocket. It feels a bit like treasure now. I found his toenail clippings in the bathroom. They suddenly looked Neolithic.

Devlin You couldn't have a lived a life together with him. I asked him once, if he could click something inside him and not need the drugs, would he do it? And he said absolutely not.

Christina I know. You came to one of his lectures, didn't you?

Devlin I did. He was brilliant. Did the image of him go at all? For a moment, anyhow?

Christina Yes. Thank you.

Devlin Liar.

Christina Sorry.

Devlin You look very melancholy. Like a renaissance pietà.

Christina I'm not a pietà, Devlin. I'm a hypocrite.

Devlin We're all hypocrites. If we weren't, there wouldn't be three pairs of friends still talking to each other in the world.

Christina Charlie's illness repulsed me. His compulsive obsession with what his prescription might be that week. Our being together was a lie.

Devlin I'm a liar too.

Christina What do you lie about?

Devlin Anything that pertains to absolutely anything. Will I go? Stay? What should I do?

Christina Whatever you want, Devlin.

Devlin No no. That would be too much.

SCENE SIX

The Space. Hodge is still sitting still. Michael and Martha are dancing to an African mass. They are holding each other close and Martha is standing on Michael's feet like the old marathon dancers. Nick walks in with a bloodied eye and nose and half a bottle of vodka in his hand. He sits and watches them. Michael tears off part of his own shirt. He takes Nick's vodka and pours a little onto the rag and bathes his cuts. Martha keeps moving to the music. She takes Nick's hand and leads him up to dance. They hold each other. Michael joins them and the three dance together closely. Hodge sits and watches. Now Martha goes to Hodge and takes him by the hand and dances close with him. Michael holds Nick tight, protective, passionate. Hodge is lost in Martha.

SCENE SEVEN

Christina's bedsit. Morning. Christina is reading Charlie's post. The door buzzes.

Christina Who is it?

Nick Nick.

She buzzes him up, opens the door and keeps reading the letters. Nick enters with a pint of milk and a packet of tea, completely trashed and bruised.

Nick Morning.

Christina Morning, Nick. God.

Nick How are you?

Christina What happened to your face?

Nick I brought you some tea. Tea.

Christina Thank you.

Nick sees the shape of a person in bed.

Have you had these cuts seen to?

Nick Who's that?

Christina Were you in a fight?

Nick Who is it?

Christina Nobody. Are you going to sit down?

Nick No. He's a cunt. Devlin's a cunt.

Christina Perhaps you should go.

Nick So you two can be on your own? Devlin, you fucker!

Nick goes to the bed and pulls the blankets off to reveal pillows.

Christina Will you have some coffee? Maybe you should go to Casualty. You might need a stitch.

Nick You could do it for me. Sew my cut.

Christina I'm not a nurse.

Nick No. You'd make a beautiful nurse, though. It'd be fantastic waking up next to you and a bowl of fruit, you know? Terrible as well. Torture if you were pulling that curtain round and I wasn't allowed to touch you. Sorry. I'll behave now. I just wanted to say you look great. Really nice. I like the way you do your hair. In a chignon.

Nick sits down. He picks up a prescription.

Did you nurse him a lot?

Christina Sometimes.

Nick How many years was he a junkie?

Christina He was an opiate-dependent.

Nick And was he on something when he died? Or was he clean?

Christina How could he be clean when he was never dirty?

Nick Is that what you think I am? Dirty?

Christina No. I think you're very drunk. And a bit confused.

Nick You're fucking beautiful.

Christina Who hit you?

Nick You did.

Christina Right.

Nick You two didn't fuck any more, did you?

Christina You should go now.

Nick Making that film. Asking me over. It was all to get through to Devlin, wasn't it? So you could reminisce about him together. You're not really going to watch that film. It's not real.

Christina Everything's real, Nick.

Nick No. Some things are real and some things we imagine. We make them up inside our head. That's where we go wrong. Things aren't clear-cut any more. That's real.

He picks up a cup and smashes it against the wall. Nick picks up a fragment and cuts the top of his arm with it.

That's real.

He puts his fingers in the blood and smears it on Christina's face.

That's real. You're so fucking beautiful. Will you put a plaster on my arm? Bathe my cut? Please?

Christina Don't. Don't do that.

Nick It's nothing, Christina. It's nothing. Please don't worry. It's fine. Sorry. We don't feel things. We don't let ourselves feel a thing. There's no sensation. And when I met you that night I felt something. I felt it. I fucking felt it. Fuck it. I still feel it. It's everywhere. In the air. It's like you're in the air. And in my blood.

He takes a bottle of water and he pours half of it over himself.

Christina I'm not. I'm not inside you. I'm not inside anyone. I don't want to be part of anyone. So why don't you just fuck off? How dare you fucking presume that you can decide things about me? Feel things about me when I haven't asked you to? Just fuck off. Leave me alone to do what I want to do.

Christina takes a cup and smashes it. She takes a piece of the debris, but before she can cut herself Nick stops her and takes the shard from her hand and holds her. He kisses her hand and holds her as she tries to push him away. There is almost a fight in how much she wants to get away and how much he wants to hold her. She cries and breaks down fully for the first time. He kneels down in front of her and puts his head to her stomach and holds her.

Nick It's alright. It's all going to be okay.

Christina Is it?

Nick It is.

He leads her to a chair and strokes her back.

Christina I killed him, Nick.

Nick No. No, you didn't.

Christina I wasn't honest with him. And you can't survive if it's a fiction.

Nick Christina. We . . . we slept together the other night. You were asleep and you thought I was Charlie. You'd smoked a lot of dope and you'd taken your sleeping pills and you . . . you thought I was him.

Christina Right.

Nick I'm sorry.

Christina Mm.

Nick Say something. Please.

Christina I watch that drunk Liam from the window. He doesn't stop walking when he crosses the road. The cars all swerve and beep at him and he just nods at them and raises his arms.

Nick I'm sorry, Christina. I'm so sorry.

Christina He reminds me of Jesus walking on water. Because maybe Galilee wasn't calm. Maybe there were broken boats and nets and waves and sewage on the lake. Who's to say that Jesus wasn't a mad pariah fucker like Liam? It's only a question of who's playing the part, isn't it? Robert Powell versus Klaus Kinski.

Nick I'm going now. I'm sorry I smashed your cup. And insulted Charlie. I didn't mean to do that. It all came out wrong. Distorted.

Christina It doesn't matter. No harm done.

Nick No. No. Have you got a dustpan and brush? I love you.

Christina Three days ago you didn't know I existed.

Nick Three days ago some people were alive and now they're dead. Things happen. There's got to be a deciding moment, hasn't there? And my moment about you was instant. Defining. Doesn't make it any less valid.

Christina I'm a bit confused, Nick. I think you probably need to go.

Nick I am. I'm going. But I'm going to come back for you. Please. In six months time. Can I come and see you? Can I do that? Please.

Christina Yes.

Nick I'm sorry I took advantage of you.

Christina You didn't. I was completely aware of both of us the other night, Nick. I didn't think for one moment that you were Charlie.

67

Nick No?

Christina No. No, I knew it was you I was with. I knew exactly who you were, Nick. I just wished you were him.

He leaves.

SCENE EIGHT

The Space. Dawn. Martha and Hodge are drinking takeaway coffees together. Hodge is drawing on a serviette.

Martha I haven't been up at dawn in a long time.

Hodge I like it. The sounds. And the all-night caffs. Are you tired?

Martha Nicely tired.

Hodge You tell me when you want to go home. I'll get you a cab.

Martha Are you wanting to sleep? Or work?

Hodge No, no. No way I'll sleep. I just meant whatever you want. Are you warm enough?

Martha I am.

Hodge You remind me of Georges Bataille, Martha.

Martha Thanks.

Hodge No. I mean how he talks about ecstasy coming into the world and being part of the atmosphere. That when you die it just comes back into the world. You give a lot. To people.

Martha Some people. You're very beautiful, Tristan.

Hodge I bet you say that to all the girls.

Martha No. I don't. I haven't found someone to be beautiful in a long time.

Hodge Oh. Well. Thanks. Tristan.

Martha What are you drawing?

Hodge I was trying to retrace the steps of how we've come to be sitting here like this. I was thinking if I could graph the map of our ending up on these chairs it would make sense.

Martha Does it have to make sense?

Hodge No. There are these fishes, Martha, who build sandcastles on the sea bed. There's about four hundred male fish to every female. So they compete for her.

Martha They make sandcastles to impress her?

Hodge Yes. They transport the sand in their mouths, so it takes them months to finish it. Then they stand next to their mound and she chooses the winner.

Martha And they swim off together.

Hodge Yeah. But these sculptures they'd made, they had such beautiful details, intricacies. Delicate joins. Can I touch your wrist? Please.

He touches Martha's wrist and forearm.

Your hand is very pure.

Martha Is it?

Hodge Isn't it?

Martha 'Who can find a virtuous woman? For her price is far above rubies.'

Hodge Bible?

Martha Proverbs.

Hodge It's like velvet. Or moss. You remind me of Leonardo's angels.

Martha I don't feel very like an angel.

Hodge I don't expect angels feel very like angels. 'Naturally love is the most distant possibility.' That's what Bataille says.

Martha cries. Hodge puts his arms around her.

Martha? I'm sorry I was quoting some French fucking thinker. I'm not very used to all this.

Martha Sorry. Sorry.

Hodge Don't be sorry. You cry, Martha. Cry as much as you want to. Did I do something wrong?

Martha No, it wasn't you.

Hodge Was it Georges Bataille? Shall I hit him for you?

Martha Tristan.

Hodge Martha.

Martha I don't think I'm who you think I am.

Hodge Well, that's fantastic.

Martha I'm a mess.

Hodge You're a beautiful mess. A beatific tangle.

Martha Sometimes I worry.

Hodge Can I do anything to take the worry away?

Martha No. Just hold my hand.

He holds her hand.

Hodge Martha.

Martha Yes.

Hodge I've never had such a night. Before.

Martha It was a wonderful night Tristan.

Hodge Will we . . . ?

Martha Will we?

Hodge Can I take you somewhere today? After you've slept. Anywhere.

Martha I need to be home. By half past three.

Hodge Before that, then. Can I take you out? Where's your favourite place?

Martha I like the river. And I like visiting the Virgin and St Anne at the National Gallery. I like to sit and watch them until they start to move.

Hodge Yeah? I used to do that, too.

Martha You can get very lost in her face.

Hodge You can. Are you hungry?

Martha I am.

Hodge I'll make up my bed for you and get some bagels from Brick Lane. Do you like bagels?

Martha I love bagels.

Hodge Oh. I'm feeling quite jealous now. Of inanimate bread objects.

Martha Can I have some coffee too?

Hodge You can. You can have anything you want.

Martha I want you.

Hodge What?

Martha You heard.

Hodge Would you say it once more? Please. For posterity.

Martha I. Want. You.

Hodge smiles, nods, kisses her wrist and leaves.

SCENE NINE

Christina's bedsit. Christina has been crying. She is pasting cuttings into a book. She sings.

Christina
  'What can I give him,
  Poor as I am?
  If I were a shepherd
  I would give a lamb.
  If I were a wise man,
  I would do my part,
  Yet what I can I give him?
  Give my heart.'

SCENE TEN

The Space. Michael and Hodge are washing the floors.

Hodge It's a waste of time.

Michael What?

Hodge The dirt's ingrained now. We need to strip it and paint it, then varnish it.

Michael We don't need to eat off it, Hodge. I got an email from East. Which paintings should we show them, do you think?

Hodge East? Yes. I just had a coffee with Martha.

Michael I don't know whether we should take along the large-scale stuff or if that would scare them off.

Hodge Where's Nick?

Michael No idea.

Hodge We haven't repainted it since we've been here.

Michael Strictly speaking you've never been here, Hodge. It's not your space. It was always mine and Nick's. You're very welcome here, you know that, but that's the way it is.

Hodge I've never wanted to be more than a collaborator. And we were discussing the floor, not who's running the place.

Michael Yeah. Exactly.

Hodge He doesn't want you.

Michael What?

Hodge Nick.

Michael What the fuck are you on about, Hodge?

Hodge It's just that I know the language of rejection. Intimately. And one fact can sometimes be more helpful than a hundred signs or clues.

Michael Thanks for the advice. I don't know what the hell you're on about. And of course you're known as Casa-fucking-nova around here, aren't you? On account of your sexual prowess.

Hodge Who called me that? Someone today?

Michael No. Nobody ever called you it.

Hodge I'm not a virgin.

Michael I'm not Elvis Presley.

Hodge No, I mean since last night. With Martha.

Michael What? Seriously?

Hodge Yeah.

Michael Fuck. Hodge. Hodge. Really? How was it?

Hodge Oh yeah, well, it was, you know . . . fantastic, yeah. Exquisite. Three times. Yeah.

Michael Christ. Shit. That's brilliant. Shit. Three times.

Hodge Yeah, yeah actually. A holy trinity. Not that I was counting.

Michael That's just fantastic.

Hodge Thanks, Mike. Yeah, she's liberated me from a lifetime of eternal carrier bags and comics.

Michael Martha's fucking gorgeous.

Hodge Yeah, well, you know.

Michael It's great. That's amazing. I'm really sorry, Hodge. I'm sorry I was a twat.

Hodge No no, that's fine.

Michael What I said about the Space. You know it's yours too. I was just being fucking mardy.

Hodge I didn't really listen to what you were saying, actually. I was just thinking about Martha.

Devlin walks in.

Devlin Who was thinking about Marta?

Hodge Nobody.

Devlin So what is this? Some sort of kabuki ritual?

Michael No. We always do it before openings.

Hodge I've got part of your fee here, Devlin.

He gives him an envelope with some notes in it and a transparent carrier bag full of small change.

They've got a machine at Sainsburys if you want to change that up. I'm getting some teas in. Do you want anything? A doughnut?

Devlin No. It will remind me that there is something missing. I took a couple of bagels from the tower someone has constructed in the kitchen. Must be a hundred of them there. It wasn't an installation, was it? I haven't eaten the art?

Michael Yeah. What the hell is that?

Hodge A tower? Oh yeah, well, maybe the mice built it.

Devlin You're very ebullient today.

Hodge Yes. I'm very hungry. I could eat a shire horse.

Martha enters.

Good morning, Martha.

Martha Hello, Hodge. What's that in the kitchen?

Hodge Do you like it?

Martha Very much. What's it called?

Hodge 'The Tower of Bagel'.

Martha And what does it represent?

Hodge It's a meditation on the notion of ecstasy. Its alternative title is 'Four Hundred Fish and She Chose Me.'

Hodge leaves and Michael follows him.

Devlin I'm sorry if I was cruel the other night, Marta. I don't remember what I said. But I suspect it was the same-old same-old. Repetitious I know. Should be like water off a swan's back to you.

Martha It was fine.

Devlin You came to find me and I wasn't here? I'm sorry if you had a sleepless night.

Martha I enjoy a sleepless night now and again..

Devlin Thank you. Benevolent as ever. I can't go through with this bloody weekend. Can you tell them for me, Marta? I'll keep the fee. I don't want them thinking well of me. I've gone to trouble anyway so technically it's mine.

Martha Where will you go?

Devlin Home. Back to exile in Bermondsey, courtesy of the Peabody Trust. I'll see you, Marta.

He kisses her forehead and starts to leave.

Martha We had a child, Devlin.

Devlin What?

Martha We have a child. I've been wanting to tell you.

Devlin What?

Martha We spent that night together in Dublin.

Devlin Yes.

Martha And I had a child.

Devlin No. You what? You had a child?

Martha I didn't tell you at the time because you'd been such an absolute bastard. Then I heard about Hildy, so I decided to tell you later.

Devlin Twelve years later.

Martha I tried to tell you. That's why I came to see you in prison. But you weren't yourself in there. You were so disorientated when I visited. I thought I'd wait until you came out. And I wrote you all those letters which you didn't reply to and I started to wonder if you needed to know about Tom.

Devlin Tom?

Martha Yeah. He's a fantastic boy. He wants to be an explorer.

Devlin We have a child.

Martha We do.

Devlin And he's called Tom.

Martha Yes. After my brother.

Devlin And he wants to be an explorer. You didn't tell me.

Martha No. We went to Sofia to find you but no one knew which part of the countryside you'd moved to. I've always talked to him about you. I told him the other day that I'd heard you were back in London. And he said he wanted to meet you.

Devlin Yes.

Martha Would you? Like to meet him?

Devlin Marta.

Martha You should, Devlin. He's a funny thing. Very intense. He loves Airfix models. His hands shake when he makes them, he's such a perfectionist.

Devlin Fucking hell, Marta.

Martha Yes, I know. Will you come round and see him? He's brilliant.

Devlin Good. That's very good. But I don't think so.

Martha You don't think so? He's not an idea, Devlin. He's a boy.

Devlin I had a child. I have no need of another. And this is hardly a fair position to put me in, Marta.

Martha You haven't any imagination, have you?

Devlin What? You're probably right. You were always right.

Martha I don't want to be right. I just want you to meet him. I couldn't care less if I never saw you again. But he wants to see you and he has that right. And meeting him could only be joyful. He's a very joyful boy.

Devlin Perhaps we could all meet the once. I could walk him round the National Gallery and explain the paintings?

Martha No. Just tea. And chips or something. At mine. Something simple.

Devlin Simple. Yes. A child.

Martha Tom. He looks at people the same way you do. The questions he asks are similar, too.

Devlin Does he drink?

Martha Not yet. He's a brilliant draughtsman.

Devlin Have you asked him to draw Giotto's perfect circle?

Martha It must have slipped my mind.

Devlin Tommy?

Martha No. Tom.

SCENE ELEVEN

Nick and Michael are in the Space, shredding papers.

Michael He's not a painter. He's a schmuck. He redefines the notion of awkward. And demanding. He wastes our time for three months. Twelve weeks we've been writing about this. Now he asks me to shred all our communications. As if anyone gives a shit what he said in his lunatic emails, anyhow. What the hell does it look like inside his head? Do you think taking up our time gives him a sense of importance?

Nick Maybe.

Michael You're not really bothered, are you?

Nick I liked meeting him.

Michael We could have met the man over a pint down the road.

Nick Do you still love painting, Michael?

Michael Course I do, yeah.

Nick Just we never seem to paint now. It's become about where it'll end up rather than what it is.

Michael We provide a brilliant space for people. Free. That's important.

Nick I said I'd stay away from her for six months.

Michael It's probably a good idea. If you can manage it.

Nick Yeah. I told her to call me if she needed to. But she hasn't.

Michael It's only been a day, Nick.

Nick Yeah. Felt like quite a long day, though. I actually think I'm going a bit mad.

Michael Go and see her. Tell her how you feel.

Nick Yeah?

Michael Get a train to Streatham. Sit down and have a quick drink in a local Firkin or Frigate or whatever. Then go and talk to her.

Nick Is that what you'd do?

Michael Yeah.

Nick Really?

Michael Yeah. Except I wouldn't need to go to Streatham to say it.

SCENE TWELVE

Christina's bedsit. Christina is knitting. A knock on the door.

Christina It's open.

Nick walks in.

Nick Hi.

Christina Hi.

Nick What you knitting?

Christina A scarf.

Nick Great. How are you?

Christina I'm a day older. You?

Nick Okay. Who's the scarf for?

Christina Devlin. He asked me to make him something.

Nick Oh.

Christina How was your day?

Nick Good. Yeah, fantastic.

Christina Painting?

Nick Shredding. Who's the scarf for?

Christina You just asked me that.

Nick Yeah. I didn't mean to ask you that. It was meant to come out as something else.

Christina Yes. Do you want some tea?

Nick No. No tea. What you been doing?

Christina Knitting. Looking out the window. I was watching the trees out there go crazy with the wind.

Nick Yeah, it's mad weather, isn't it?

Christina I've been watching people. Walking down the road. It's been cold, hasn't it?

Nick Freezing. The space is like an igloo.

Christina Do you cut holes in the middle of the floor and look for fish?

Nick Yeah. And we've got a couple of seals in the corner too.

Christina Good.

Nick Christina. I need to know if . . . No no, I don't need to know anything.

Christina If what?

Nick Nothing. I'm not asking you for anything. Not now. Not for ages. I just wondered if I should wait for you? If you'd like me to wait.

Christina Does it have to be a definite yes or no?

Nick Yes. Unless it's a no, in which case it can be a variation.

Christina Nick . . .

Nick Christina.

Christina I do find it very hard to accept love. I do. Find it hard.

Nick That's okay. The important things aren't easy, are they? I mean, I support Southampton. That's not always easy.

Christina Isn't it?

Nick No. It's fucking heartbreaking. So is there hope?

Christina There's always hope.

Nick No. No, there isn't.

Christina In this case there's hope.

Nick Devlin was reading us some of Rumi's poems. One of them said that God made Majnun love Layla so much that even her dog caused confusion in him.

Christina That's nice.

Nick Yeah. Even her dog.

SCENE THIRTEEN

The Space. Michael is at his computer. He listens to a tape on his Dictaphone and repeats the Arabic phrases.

Tape Leave me alone. *Utruknee waHdee.*

Michael *Utruknee waHdee.*

Tape I'm ill. *Ana mareeD.*

Michael *Ana mareeD.*

Tape I'm lost. *Ana tuht.*

Michael *Ana tuht.*

Tape Where are the bathrooms? *Ayn al-Hammaamaat.*

Michael *Ayn al- Hammaamaat.*

SCENE FOURTEEN

Martha and Devlin are in a street.

Devlin What's he run off for?

Martha He wanted to buy you a present. With his pocket money.

Devlin Tell him next time I'd just prefer the pocket money.

Martha How was it for you?

Devlin Did you tell him to do that? To call me Dad?

Martha Course I didn't.

Devlin Chasing me round the Brueghel rooms shouting 'Dad ! What's that, Dad?' It was surreal, Marta.

Martha It's lovely that he can be so open. People must have thought you were the paragon of a parent.

Devlin He'd never heard of Giotto. What have you been teaching him?

Martha A lot of useless information. Do you like him, Devlin?

Devlin What kind of a stupid question is that?

Martha Do you?

Devlin He's everything, isn't he? Beauty. Innocence. Spirit. How could one not like him?

Martha So you'll see him again?

Devlin If he wants to see me. But it's his choice, of course.

Martha I think he will want to see you.

Devlin Do you? Do you think so?

Martha Yes. I do. He was talking about it.

Devlin Right. Good. I'm not taking him to see those fucking sharks at the aquarium, though. Huge white death's heads.

Martha They are in tanks, Devlin.

Devlin Everything's fallible, Marta. He's inherited your looks. Poor fella might have my nose, though.

Martha Your nose is very fine.

Devlin Is it? It's not bad, is it? It's better seen from the left, actually. I told him I couldn't paint any more. He was so intelligent about it. Incisive.

Martha What did he say?

Devlin He just nodded. We sat there saying nothing for a bit. Then he put his arm around me for a moment. Like a monkey. With his red backpack.

He takes Martha's hand.

Martha Do you think we'll ever stop, Devlin?

Devlin Stop what?

Martha Stop trying. Do you think we'll ever stop trying and just be ourselves?

Devlin Surely the act of trying is being ourselves.

Martha No. I don't think it is. But trying's rather beautiful in itself, isn't it?

Devlin It is. Marta. It is.

Martha Martha.

Devlin Martha.

Martha Martha.

Lights down.